MEG

TILLY

EMILY

PAPER TABS

Welcome to Paper Dolls...

Meet Meg, Tilly and Emily - three fashion - loving paper dolls! Cut out each full size paper doll and each outfits, including the paper tabs.
Then simply fold each tab to place the clothes onto your dolls. You may need an adult to help with cutting! Then place your dressed up dolls in the scenes at the back of the book.

Savvy Stationery

Copyright © 2022 Savvy Stationery

All rights reserved. No portion of this book may be reproduced in any form without permission from the publisher, except as permitted by U.S. copyright law

Meg's Outfits

Meg's Outfits

Meg's Outfits

Tilly's Outfits

Tilly's Outfits

Tilly's Outfits

Tilly's Outfits

Emily's Outfits

Emily's Outfits

Emily's Outfits

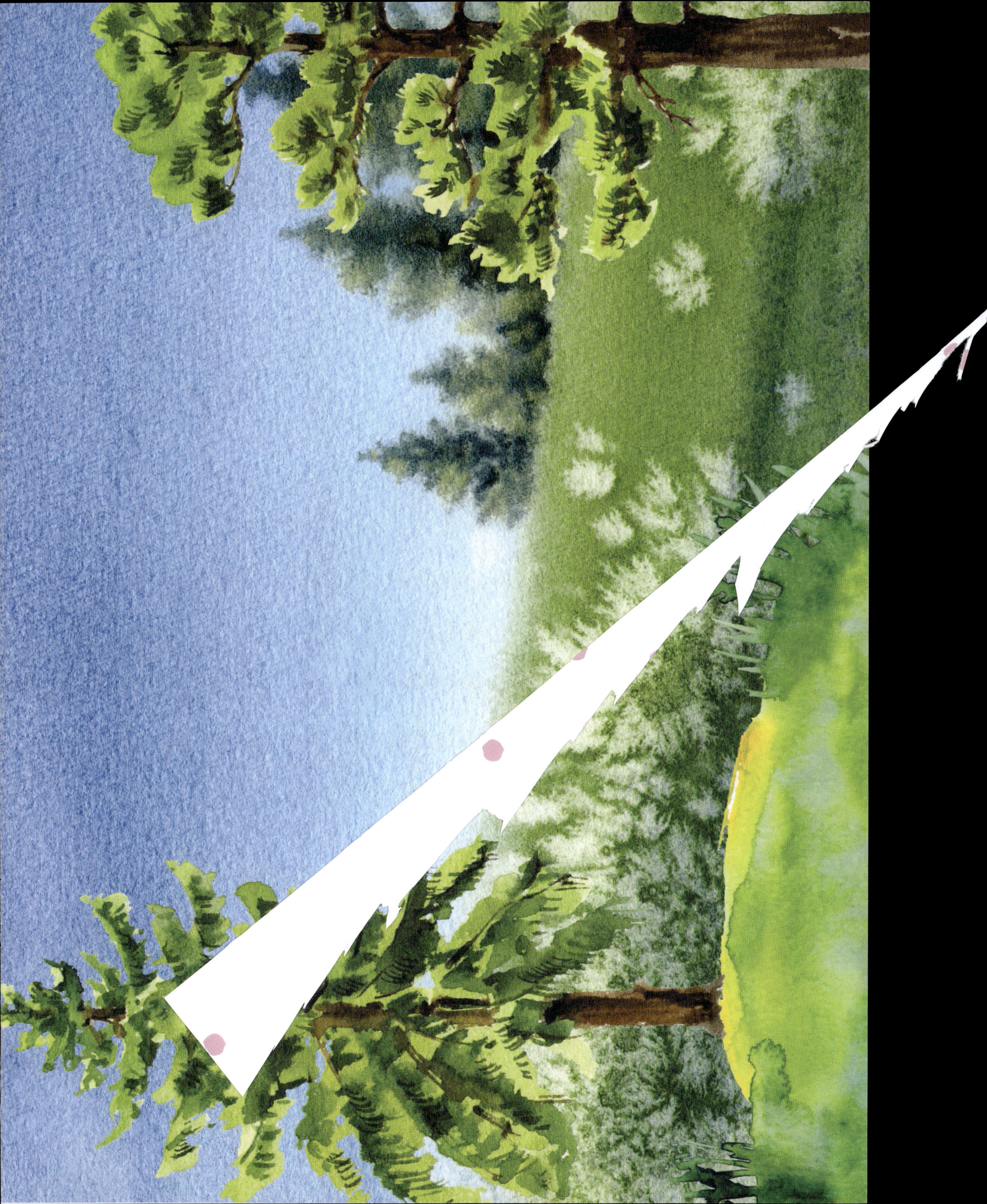

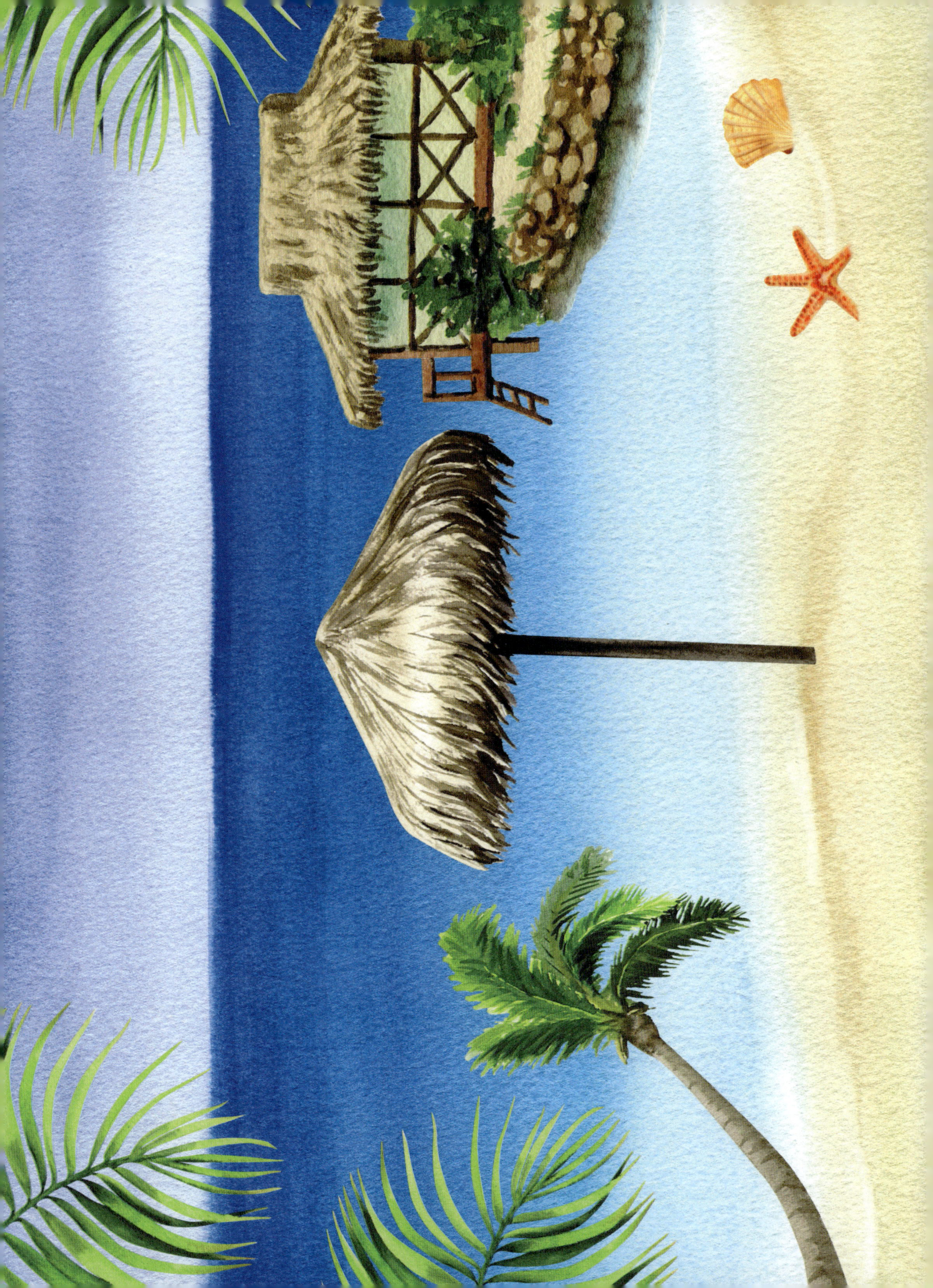

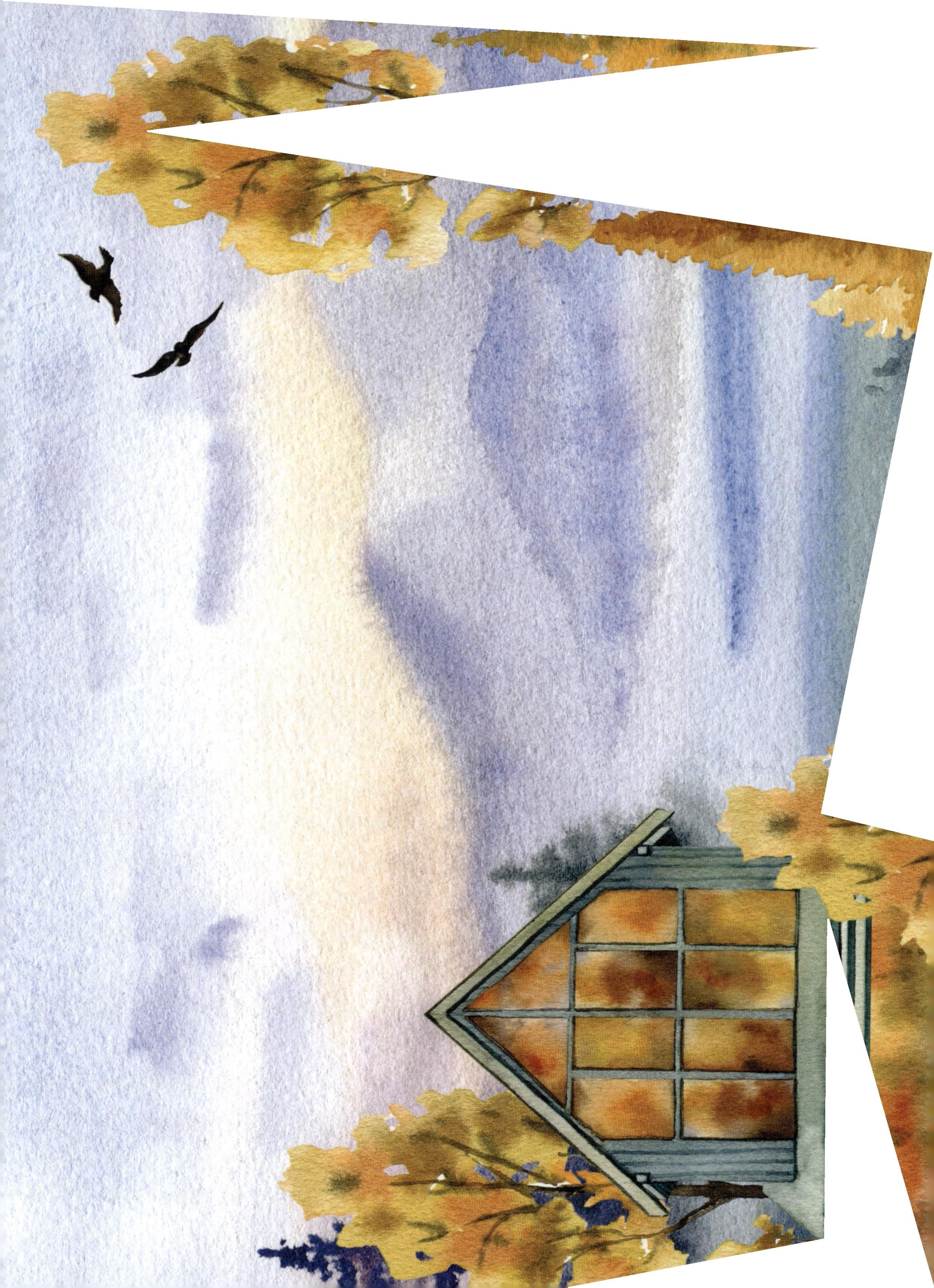

Printed in Great Britain
by Amazon